A Kid's Guide to MYTHOLOGY

ATHENA

TAMMY GAGNE

Mitchell Lane

PUBLISHERS
P.O. Box 196
Hockessin, DE 19707
www.mitchelllane.com

Mitchell Lane
PUBLISHERS

Printing   1   2   3   4   5   6   7   8

A Kid's Guide to MYTHOLOGY

Apollo
Athena
Hercules
Jason

Odysseus
Poseidon
Thor
Zeus

Library of Congress Cataloging-in-Publication Data
Gagne, Tammy, author.
 Athena / by Tammy Gagne.
    pages cm. — (A kid's guide to mythology)
 Summary: "When the ancient Greeks found themselves in a difficult situation, they would pray to this daughter of Zeus for guidance. Of course, like the other gods and goddesses, Athena was not without faults. Her fierce independence often led her to rebel against her father and to fight with her many brothers and sisters. But she also came to their aid over and over again, proving herself to be worthy of her title--and all the respect with which it came" — Provided by publisher.
 Audience: Age 8–11.
 Audience: Grades 3–6.
 Includes bibliographical references and index.
 ISBN 978-1-61228-998-4 (library bound)
 1. Athena (Greek deity)—Juvenile literature. 2. Mythology, Greek—Juvenile literature.
 3. Gods, Greek—Juvenile literature. 4. Mythology in literature—Juvenile literature. I. Title.
 BL820.M6G34 2016
 398.20938'01—dc23
                                                                            2015005442
eBook ISBN: 978-1-61228-999-1

PUBLISHER'S NOTE: The Internet sites referenced herein were active as of the publication date. Due to the fleeting nature of some web sites, we cannot guarantee they will all be active when you are reading this book.

To reflect current usage, we have chosen to use the secular era designations BCE ("before the common era") and CE ("of the common era") instead of the traditional designations BC ("before Christ") and AD (anno Domini, "in the year of the Lord").

DISCLAIMER: Many versions of each myth exist today. The author is covering only one version of each story. Other versions may differ in details.

CONTENTS

Words in **bold** throughout can be found in the Glossary.

Statues of Athena can be found throughout the world. This one, built between 1893 and 1902, stands in front of parliament in Vienna, Austria. Athena holds a spear in her left hand while Nike, the winged goddess of victory, stands in her right hand.

ATHENA'S GIFT

Grocery shopping was Erin's least favorite pastime. Luckily her mother let her bring her best friend Lily along this time. Having a friend to talk to seemed to make the time go by more quickly. And Erin and Lily always had the best conversations. This time they were discussing superpowers.

"If you could have one superpower—anything at all—what would it be?" Lily asked as Erin rolled the cart through the produce section.

"Hmmm," Erin said as they neared the spinach. "Maybe the power to make green vegetables taste like chocolate!" Lily laughed. "How about you?" Erin asked.

"I'd want to be the most beautiful woman in the world," Lily decided. "Think about it. I could have everything I wanted."

"Nah," Erin responded. "Being beautiful wouldn't get you *everything* you wanted. Besides, how would you know when people liked you for you and not just for your looks? I'd want to be the smartest woman in the world," she decided.

"Sounds like you girls should read about Athena (uh-THEE-nuh)," interjected a familiar-looking lady peering over the tomatoes. It was Ms. Brasslow, the librarian from their school. "Do you know much about the Greek goddesses?" she asked the girls as she continued to make her selections.

At first the girls were startled by Ms. Brasslow's question. They didn't realize anyone had been listening to them. But they quickly welcomed her into their debate. Ms. Brasslow was one of their favorite people. She always recommended the best books.

The girls shook their heads no before asking, "Who's Athena?" at the same time.

"Athena is the goddess of wisdom," explained Ms. Brasslow. "That gal definitely knows a thing or two about using her brain to get what she wants." It seemed the librarian was taking Erin's side—at least at first. But then she added, "The goddess of beauty is Aphrodite (aff-ruh-DAHY-tee). You should read up on her as well. Come to the library during your free period tomorrow. I'll introduce you to both of them."

Beauty *and* Brains

They started with Aphrodite, perhaps because she came first alphabetically. In every book Ms. Brasslow showed them Aphrodite indeed looked beautiful. Every drawing showed her with flawless skin and long, blond hair. But the more they read, the less attractive Aphrodite became. She was still pretty on the outside, of course. On the inside, though, she was terribly vain. She was also extremely jealous. She reminded them of the mean girls at school who thought they were better than everyone else.

"I wouldn't want to be like her," Lily realized aloud.

Athena, on the other hand, was a whole different story. Instead of feeling envious of others, she inspired those who worshipped her to be brave and resourceful like she was. She wasn't as pretty as Aphrodite. But she was striking in other ways. She is said to have had piercing grey eyes. She also wore a **plumed** helmet and carried a shield. This represented her role as a protector of the ancient Greeks. Many drawings depicted her with an owl on her shoulder or a coiled snake at her feet. Athena was also a clever inventor. She is said to have created numbers, musical instruments like the flute and trumpet, and the plow. Just the way she carried herself made her look strong and confident, which was beautiful in a way that Aphrodite just couldn't manage.

A Gift That Kept Giving

Even some of the gods themselves were envious of Athena. One of them was Poseidon (poh-SAHYD-un), god of the sea. The two were said to have engaged in a contest in ancient Greece. Both Athena and Poseidon wanted to rule a special city by the sea. Being the god of the sea, Poseidon thought it only natural that he be the city's ruler. But in addition to being wise, Athena was also determined. She knew that she could win the ancients over. "Let's allow the people to choose which one of us they prefer," the goddess suggested.

Poseidon slammed his mighty **trident** to the ground, instantly creating a magnificent fountain. He promised the people that if they chose him, they would always have water. He also pledged to fill the nearby ocean with fish and keep the sailors safe on the water. He was certain his wondrous gift would ensure his victory. The people were excited—until they realized that the salty water was undrinkable. Athena then took her turn. She stamped her foot and from the dust an olive tree grew right before everyone's eyes.

Comparing the gifts, the people immediately saw how much more the tree offered them. Not only could the people eat the olives, but they could also use the oil to cook and fuel their lamps, and use the tree itself for shade. Since ancient times the olive tree has become an important symbol of life in Greece.

When the people voted, the results were close. The men preferred Poseidon's gift; the women preferred Athena's olive tree. And as it happened there was one more woman voting than men—a fact that Athena likely knew when she suggested the vote.

Known for his horrid temper, Poseidon became enraged. Just as he had used his trident to create the fountain, he now pointed it toward the sky. A terrible storm appeared out of nowhere, threatening the people. But Athena protected them. They gathered underneath her olive tree until the last drop of rain had fallen. Poseidon had thought he was punishing them. But he had actually shown them that they had made the better decision.

The people celebrated by naming their city Athens, after their ruling goddess Athena. They also built a wondrous temple in her honor. Inside it stood an ivory and gold statue of the goddess. It was seven times taller than the average man. To help ensure that Poseidon wouldn't become angry again, they also built a smaller temple in his honor. Today most people view the myths about Athena and Poseidon as mere stories. But the temples are undeniably real. Numerous structures were in fact built to pay tribute to the Greek gods and goddesses. Some still stand today.

AN ANCIENT REPLACEMENT

The first temple built for Athena was destroyed when the Persians invaded Greece in 480 BCE. But another soon took its place: the Parthenon was built to replace the original. Construction began in 447 BCE and continued for nine years. The structure, which included eight outer columns along the front and another eight along the back, had seventeen outer columns on each side. Sculptures of Athena, Poseidon, and others decorated the outside of the monument. An olive tree was paired with one of the likenesses of Athena. Poseidon's figure was seen with his trident. The Parthenon can still be seen in Athens, though it's a bit weathered from time. Many of the sculptures are now housed in the British Museum in London, England.

The sculptures include metopes, squares of carved marble which were placed along the top of the Parthenon on all four sides. There were originally over one hundred of these squares, showing a parade of men, women, children, and animals. No one is certain what these carvings represent. Some say they illustrate the founding of Athens. Others think they show the gods, goddesses, and citizens of Athens at the Panathenaea (pan-ath-uh-NEE-uh). This event, which honored Athena, was held every four years in Athens. The Panathenaea included athletic competitions like the Olympic Games. But it also featured musical contests and poetry—and even a few athletic events that the Olympics did not.

Parthenon

Athena and her Roman counterpart Minerva also appear in many paintings. This one, finished in 1668, shows Minerva crowning Apollo, the god of light and music.

STORIES STILL TOLD

The gods and goddesses were the center of the ancient Greeks' religion. A person faced with a difficult decision would pray to Athena for wisdom and guidance. Likewise, a mother would pray to Athena to keep her son safe as he went to war. The wives of fishermen would pray to Poseidon to protect them on their journeys. And a person who needed to get in touch with a distant loved one would pray to Hermes (HUR-meez), the messenger of the gods. It seemed that there was a god or goddess for everything.

But how did the stories about all of these gods and goddesses come to be? And why did the ancient Greeks believe in them so deeply? It is important to remember that science has come a long way over the last 2,500 years. In ancient Greece, the people didn't know how the solar system worked. They had no idea that the earth orbited the sun, for example. They created a myth to explain how the sun rose each morning and set each evening. A god named Apollo (uh-POL-oh) was given credit for this particular **phenomenon**. But instead of directing the earth around the sun, he was said to pull the sun across the sky each day with his golden chariot. The people would pray to Apollo if they wanted a sunny day for an important outdoor event.

Family Relations

Athena and Apollo are actually half-siblings. They have the same father, Zeus (ZOOS). But Apollo's mother is Leto (LEE-toh), while Athena's mother is Metis (MEE-tis). When Metis became pregnant with Athena, Zeus's grandparents told him that the child would be braver and wiser than he was. This scared him so much that he tricked Metis into turning herself into a fly and swallowed her at once.

Zeus thought this act would prevent the child from being born. But soon his head began throbbing. When the pain got worse, he ordered his son Hephaestus (hi-FES-tuhs) to cut his skull open. Zeus hoped that by doing so he would relieve his pain. But instead, a full-grown goddess emerged. That goddess was Athena. It was no accident that she was born from her father's head. This first myth about the goddess is a symbol of her powerful mind.

It's a Long Story

Greek gods and goddesses have been featured in some of the oldest stories ever told. One of those stories is an epic poem called the *Iliad*. The word epic has come to be a slang term meaning "spectacular" in our modern vocabulary. And that definition is not entirely off base when it comes to this revered piece of literature. But when it comes to poetry, the word epic actually refers to the length of the work. The *Iliad* is more than fifteen thousand lines long. Most people think that this poem was written by an ancient **bard** named Homer. In ancient Greece bards would travel throughout the land reciting poems as

The birth of Athena is a symbol of her intelligent mind. The goddess was born fully grown from the skull of her father, Zeus.

they played music. Like the *Iliad*, these poems usually told stories. This story was about the end of the Trojan War.

Athena's part of the story begins before the start of the war, however. At the beginning of the myth, Athena, Hera (HEER-uh), and Aphrodite are attending a wedding on Mount Olympus. Another goddess named Eris (ER-iss) is not invited to the celebration, however. Being overlooked naturally makes Eris very angry. And as the goddess of **discord**, she decides to get revenge by causing some trouble. In the middle of the festivities, Eris shows up and throws down a golden apple with the phrase "to the fairest" inscribed on it. In ancient times the word *fairest* was another way of saying "most beautiful." Eris knew that this simple act would turn the happy occasion into one filled with conflict.

Just as Eris hoped, the apple immediately draws the attention of several goddesses. Athena, Hera, and Aphrodite all try to claim the prize. But of course, only one can be the fairest. To decide who it will be, they take part in a rather strange beauty contest. "Zeus, chief god and Hera's husband, knew better than to get involved," writes journalist Frank Whelan. "So the goddesses asked Trojan Prince Paris to judge."[1] All three of them want to be named the fairest goddess so badly that they bribe Paris with their unique and powerful abilities.

Athena promises the prince wisdom and skill if he chooses her. With it he could surely win any war. Hera, the queen of all the gods, offers to make him the king of all the land in Europe and Asia instead. With that he would surely be the richest man on earth. Aphrodite, however, offers him something that he finds even more tempting: the love of the most beautiful woman in the world— Helen. "She keeps her part of the bargain and helps him lure Helen," continues Whelan. "That Helen is already married to Menelaus (men-ul-EY-uhs), King of Sparta, does not bother Aphrodite."[2] All she cares about is winning the golden apple.

When Paris brings Helen back to Troy with him, the move sparks the Trojan War. Athena also plays an important part in this war. She **resents** Paris for not choosing her in the contest at Mount Olympus. She also develops a fierce dislike of Aphrodite—and an outright hatred for the Trojans. A Trojan priestess named

This painting, The Judgment of Paris, was created in 1480. It shows the Trojan prince deciding whether Athena, Hera, or Aphrodite would receive the golden apple and be named "the fairest."

Theano (thay-ah-NOH) prays to Athena to save Troy during the war. But Athena has no interest in helping the Trojans. The goddess even goes as far as to say, "Let [the Trojan prince] Hector die a thousand deaths!"[3]

Learning from Mistakes

Homer refers to Athena as the "guard of the armies of Zeus" in the war.[4] She and Hera set their differences over the apple aside for the sake of the Greek people. They work together, sometimes even against the wishes of Zeus. "As Zeus mocked them, [Athena and Hera] huddled together to continue plotting Troy's destruction," Homer recited.[5] This disregard shows that Athena's confidence is both her biggest strength and her greatest weakness. She clearly thinks she knows better than anyone, even more than the king of the gods and goddesses.

At one point Zeus forbids the gods and goddesses from interfering in the war. He alone wants to control the outcome. But Athena and Hera ignore him and start off in their chariot to earth nonetheless. Zeus becomes furious. "Let her find out what it means to fight against her father," he declares.[6]

Athena is a complicated character in the *Iliad*. At times her choices make it seem like she completely disrespects Zeus. But at other times she seems to feel sorry for her **rebellious** actions. At the very least she is sad to have disappointed him. "Zeus hates me now," she exclaims when she reflects on his disapproval. "I want to be his darling grey-eyed girl again."[7] It won't be the last time that Athena insists on interfering with happenings on Earth, though.

HELPING HERCULES

Hercules is widely known for his strength. But as they say, behind every great god is a smart goddess. In the case of Hercules, Athena made all the difference when it came to a most troubling time. Hera proved to be a vicious enemy to her stepson, Hercules. At one point she even caused him to lose his mind. In an angry and confused fit, he killed his own wife and children. While Hera had been behind the breakdown, Hercules had to pay for his actions nonetheless.

His punishment was to serve as a slave to King Eurystheus (yoo-RIS-thee-uhs) for twelve years. During this time the king assigned Hercules the Twelve Labors. These challenges were so difficult that other men—and even gods—would have found them impossible. But if he wanted forgiveness, Hercules had to perform them.

Athena helped Hercules in many ways. When the king instructed him to drive an enormous flock of birds from a nearby lake, she provided Hercules with magical noisemakers. When he needed to skin the Nemean lion, Athena instructed him to use the lion's own claws to tear through its thick skin. And when his final challenge took Hercules to the underworld, Athena was there to guide him. But one of the biggest ways Athena helped Hercules took place even before these challenges began. When the goddess discovered what Hercules had done to his wife and children, she knocked him out at once. This effectively ended his killing spree so that he could harm no one else.

Hercules

The Odyssey, *Homer's* sequel to the Iliad, *tells the story of the Greek war hero Odysseus who spends a decade traveling home after the Trojan War. Athena admires Odysseus and protects him during his journey.*

A LONG JOURNEY HOME

Athena also plays a significant role in another famous poem by Homer. One might call the *Odyssey* the sequel to the *Iliad*. This only slightly shorter poem picks up where the *Iliad* leaves off. It tells the story of a Greek soldier named Odysseus (oh-DIS-ee-uhs) as he travels home after the Trojan War. Like the poem itself, the journey is long. It takes Odysseus ten years. And many exciting adventures occur on his way. He encounters one-eyed monsters called Cyclopes, horrendous storms, and even some of the Greek gods themselves.

At the beginning of the *Odyssey*, the reader sees a softer side to Athena. Feeling sorry for Odysseus, she begs Zeus to allow her to help him find his way home after all the fighting he has endured. "My own heart is broken for Odysseus," she tells Zeus.[1] But Athena's soft spot for Odysseus doesn't lessen her own strength. Instead, it inspires her to do everything she can to help the war hero make his way back to his home on the island of Ithaca (ITH-uh-kuh).

Odysseus's journey home took him from Troy, in modern-day Turkey, to Ithaca in Greece. Athens, the city that Athena protects, is located between the two.

Changing Appearances

While Athena relies on her wisdom, she clearly understands that many humans regard an attractive appearance as important. Perhaps this understanding comes from seeing Aphrodite succeed at influencing people with her beauty. But remember, Athena is much smarter than her fellow goddess. She is also devious. One of the ways she helps Odysseus is by making him more handsome. She knows that the people he meets along his way will be more likely to help him as a result.

Athena disguises herself as a variety of different people to help guide Odysseus. But eventually, she comes to him in her true form. "Two of a kind, we are, **contrivers**, both," she tells him at this time. "Of all the men alive you are the

Odysseus encountered many obstacles during his long journey home. While at sea, he passed the Sirens. These creatures' beautiful voices had lured many sailors toward their island, only to have their boats wrecked on the rocky coastline. Odysseus plugged his men's ears with wax and ordered them to tie him up until they had safely passed the Sirens.

best in plots and story telling. My own fame is for wisdom among the gods—**deceptions** too. Would even you have guessed that I am Pallas Athena, daughter of Zeus, I that am always with you in times of **trial**, a shield to you in battle?"[2]

Athena's words don't just reveal her identity to Odysseus. They also reveal the reason for her strong attachment to Odysseus. Athena sees the two of them as having much in common. This also explains why she disobeys Zeus at times even though she wants to please him. Athena sees action as being an important weapon.

And she is willing to act for a greater good when necessary, even if it means deceiving or disobeying at times.

By the end of the *Odyssey*, the reader learns even more about Athena. Odysseus arrives home to find that a number of men have tried to convince his wife to marry them in his absence. Odysseus kills the men with Athena's help. The men's families soon hear of what has happened and set out for revenge. But Athena prevents an endless cycle of bloodshed from occurring. "This gruesome war has lasted long enough" she cries. "Stop now, shed no more blood, and stand apart."[3]

Homer stated, "The townsmen heard; and pale with fear, they lost their weapons: spears and swords flew from their hands, dropped to the ground—the goddess's voice had terrifying force. They wheeled back, toward the city, **keen** to live. . . . Then patient, bright Odysseus's battle cry was **savage**, like an eagle from on high. . . ."[4]

Athena once again intervenes. "Halt now; [end] this relentless war, lest you [anger] Zeus," she warns.[5] And again, despite her earlier disobedience, she shows a definite respect for Zeus. But it is important to note that Odysseus obeys Athena, not the king of the gods. Here, once again, she proves that her power at times rivals that of Zeus himself. Following his wishes, she is the one who actually accomplishes the goal.

Stories That Still Matter

To some kids—and even some adults—mythology may at first seem outdated. You may even wonder why these ancient stories are still being told. Journalist Kevin Canfield explains that many of the stories we think of as modern and original are actually based on Greek mythology.

Ancient Greek stories are still important in the modern world. This Greek stamp, printed in 1983, shows Odysseus killing the men who have tried to marry his wife.

"[W]hen you think about it, what isn't based on Greek mythology these days?" he asks. "Take, for example . . . *O Brother, Where Art Thou?*, a film that its creators, Ethan and Joel Coen, say is based on the *Odyssey*. Though some critics and scholars see little evidence of a link between Homer's epic and the film, there was apparently enough of one to [earn] the film an Oscar nomination for best adapted screenplay."[6]

Canfield also notes that the wildly popular Harry Potter books and movies draw from Greek mythology. "The series features several characters—including Hermione Granger and Argus Filch—named after and, to a certain extent, modeled on Greek mythic figures."[7] In Greek mythology, Argus Panoptes is a hundred-eyed giant, while Helen of Troy's daughter is named Hermione. Hogwarts Professor McGonagall also shares her first name with Athena's Roman **counterpart**, Minerva.

University of Connecticut professor Roger Travis points out that mythology is a unique part of culture. For one thing, it seems to bridge the gap between the rich and the poor. Myths are popular with people of all walks of life, nearly everywhere. He thinks that people rely on

Emma Watson appears here in the 2007 movie Harry Potter and the Order of the Phoenix. Her character Hermione Granger shares a name with the daughter of Helen of Troy. Minerva McGonagall, one of Harry and Hermione's professors, was named for Athena's Roman counterpart.

these kinds of stories today nearly as much as they did thousands of years ago. "This mode of story—violent things like curses and people in great power doing horrible things and getting punished for it—it's a story that human beings need to tell themselves and each other."[8]

Travis teaches a class called Classical Mythology. Even though the subject matter is old, he often uses modern films as examples of the themes found in mythology. "[M]ost of what was myth for the Greeks and is really still myth for us can be found in popular culture, and storytelling in popular culture is mostly in the movies."[9]

ATHENA, THE ROLE MODEL

The name Athena has become a symbol of powerful women everywhere. A shining example is the Athena Film Festival in New York City. The annual event celebrates the work of female filmmakers. In 2011, women made up 5 percent of the directors in Hollywood. "That is a kick in the gut," says Melissa Silverstein, co-founder of the festival.[10] Add in other behind-the-scenes jobs, and the numbers aren't much better. Overall women make up about 18 percent of these jobs in the film business.

Trudie Styler is an actress and the co-owner of a production company called Maven Films. Styler and her business partner Celine Rattray started the company to focus on female talent—from actresses to writers and directors. "We're not making some angry stand," Styler points out. "But we are two female filmmakers in what is a male industry, and so we're very supportive of female-driven projects . . . there's a **plethora** of actresses out there who are looking for meatier roles and we're reaping the benefits of that."[11]

Silverstein adds that she hopes to change the widely held idea that women in Hollywood can't succeed if they help each other out. "There is a mythology that women can't be friends with each other because they have to compete for jobs. We have to get beyond that," she insists.[12]

Trudie Styler

25

Athena still plays a part in many modern stories. In the Percy Jackson book and movie series, Alexandra Daddario plays Annabeth Chase, Athena's demigoddess daughter. The character shares many of her mother's powerful traits.

PASSING HER
WISDOM DOWN

Today Greek mythology serves many purposes. People still read these stories with great interest and enthusiasm. Some of the stories have even been made into movies, television shows, and comic books. Many versions simply retell the old myths while others use the original myths as a jumping-off point for new tales. One enormously successful version of Greek mythology is the Percy Jackson book and film series. Written by Rick Riordan, these modern stories tell of the adventures of a new generation of gods—or **demigods** rather. They are the children of Athena, Poseidon, and the other Greek gods. While each child has a god or goddess as one of their parents, the other parent is a human.

Like Mother, Like Daughter

In Riordan's stories, Athena's daughter is Annabeth Chase. Alexandra Daddario plays the film version of the demigoddess. Like her mother, Annabeth is smart and strong. One might think that playing such a powerful character would be difficult. But Daddario didn't see it that way. "It was more empowering than challenging," she notes. "The challenges involved the physical training that we had. We had a lot of fight **choreography**, and you have to work out a lot, so make sure you're in shape. That kind of thing. So you get really tired. It was really cool. You feel really tough and **empowered** and you bring out a side of you that you didn't know existed. Like I don't get to go around sword fighting with people in my normal life, and I get to sword fight with people in the movie. That's pretty cool."[1]

Annabeth doesn't spend much time with her mother. But she does have a big scene with one of Athena's worst enemies, Medusa (muh-DOO-suh). Athena played a large part in shaping the image of this evil creature. According to the myth, though, Medusa wasn't always ugly. She started out as a beautiful, blond priestess of Athena. Like

The frightening Medusa appears in both the oldest Greek myths and the more recent Percy Jackson movie series. She is no match for the clever daughter of Athena, however.

all priestesses, Medusa had promised never to marry. But when she caught the eye of Poseidon, Medusa was thrilled to have his attention. Eventually, she broke her vow so she could be with him.

Feeling betrayed and angry, Athena decided to punish the maiden by taking the very thing that had attracted Poseidon—Medusa's beauty. The goddess transformed Medusa's long golden locks into **venomous** snakes. She changed her loving eyes into magical orbs that would bring tragedy to those who looked into them. Anyone who dared look Medusa in the eye would immediately be turned to stone. The story became a warning about vanity and the cost of breaking one's word.

Using Her Head

Daddario thinks that many important messages come through in both the Percy Jackson books and films. "Greek myths are sort of like lessons also. Sometimes it's not the most obvious thing to overcome an option. Like the **Hydra**, it would be obvious just to cut off all of its heads or look at Medusa to kill her, but sometimes there's a different way that you have to go to overcome the difficult things. . . . If at first it doesn't come, try again."[2]

Wisdom and strength aren't the only things that Annabeth inherits from her goddess mother. She also possesses a natural suspicion of Aphrodite. In *The Mark of Athena*, Annabeth immediately feels uneasy when she encounters the goddess. "The woman was breathtakingly beautiful and strangely familiar," writes Riordan. "Her face was hard to describe. Her features seemed to shift from those of one glamorous movie star to another. Her eyes sparkled playfully—sometimes green or blue or amber. Her

In Greek mythology the Hydra was a nine-headed water serpent. When anyone cut off one of the heads, two more would grow back in its place.

hair changed from long, straight blond to dark chocolatey curls. . . . Annabeth was instantly jealous."[3]

Unlike Athena, though, her daughter seems more aware that her envy could lead her into trouble. "Everything about her seemed calculated to make Annabeth feel **inadequate** . . . Annabeth realized that her jealousy was **irrational**. The woman was making her feel this way. She'd had this experience before. She recognized this woman, even though her face changed by the second, becoming more and more beautiful. 'Aphrodite,' she said."[4]

Outwitting Her Enemies

Many myths about Athena center on the downfalls of beauty and pride. One such story focuses on Athena and a weaver named Arachne (uh-RAK-nee). The weaver herself

wasn't especially beautiful. But her work was breathtaking. And she knew it. Thinking that no one could match the images she created, she challenged Athena to a weaving contest.

Athena's work was pretty enough. She wove an image of the Parthenon and the contest she'd had with Poseidon. Arachne's images were much more dazzling. She decided to use the opportunity to embarrass the gods. Trying to make Athena and her family look bad, Arachne spun images that highlighted the gods' and goddesses' fears and weaknesses. Her work was still striking. But it was also mean spirited.

Athena pointed this out. But she also told Arachne that her love for her work was obvious. Because of that fact, she said, she would make it possible for Arachne to continue spinning for the rest of her days. By sprinkling the weaver with magical herbs, she turned her into a tiny, ugly creature that we know today as a spider. Athena might not have woven better than Arachne. But she had definitely outwitted her.

Athena's sharp mind is the driving force in both the myths about her and the modern tales of which she is now a part. When Annabeth becomes frustrated at her own lack of powers, her mother's words echo in her head. "'You've got your intelligence,' a voice said. Annabeth wondered if Athena was speaking to her, but that was probably just wishful thinking. Intelligence . . . like Athena's favorite hero, Odysseus. He'd won the Trojan War with cleverness, not strength. He had overcome all sorts of monsters and hardships with his quick wits. That's what Athena valued."[5]

Slowly, Annabeth was remembering how her own most important gift worked. *"Wisdom's daughter walks*

alone. . . . That didn't mean just without other people, Annabeth realized. It meant without any special powers."[6] One might say that Riordan's demigod characters learn the lessons that even the gods and goddesses of the original mythology did not. Perhaps one of the reasons his modern myths play out so well is because his characters are half human, after all.

Many Greek myths explain how different parts of nature came to exist. The story of the weaving competition between Athena and Arachne offers an interesting take on how the spider was created.

ALL GREEK TO ME

"Monsters, gods, and heroes [are] all surefire favorites in the classroom," according to the National Endowment for the Humanities. "But Greek mythology offers so much more: inspiration for many works of art (both written and visual), insight into the human condition, a glimpse at an ancient people trying to make sense of phenomena they could not explain, and the source for many names and terms we use today. [You] might be surprised to find [you're] wearing shoes with the name of a Greek goddess (Nike), rooting for (or against) a team named after Greek gods (Tennessee Titans), and even listening to rock groups with mythological names (Styx)."[7]

The way people speak has been influenced by Greek—and the related Roman -myths, too. The English language is peppered with words with mythological origins. The word *panic*, for example, comes from the Greek shepherd god named Pan. You might know that the colored part of your eye is called the *iris*. But did you know that Iris is the Greek goddess of the rainbow? Did you eat *cereal* for breakfast this morning? This word too has an origin from mythology. Ceres (SEER-eez) is the Roman goddess of grain.

Iris

The Parthenon still stands in Athens—although it looks a bit different today than it did when it was completed in 438 BCE.

5

WORKS OF ART

Anyone who visits modern-day Athens can see that the spirit of Athena lives on in the city. The ancient Greeks built many statues and monuments to honor their favorite goddess. The people and Athena were so closely linked that it can be hard to separate them when considering some of the larger structures, such as the Parthenon.

Jeffrey Hurwit is a professor of art history at the University of Oregon and an expert on the art and architecture of the ancient Greeks. As he explains, "The Parthenon was the greatest monument in the greatest sanctuary of the greatest city of classical Greece. It was the central **repository** of the Athenians' very lofty [beliefs about] themselves. It was the physical, marble **embodiment** of their values, of their beliefs, of their myths. . . . And it was thus as much a temple to Athens and the Athenians as it was to their . . . goddess, Athena herself. Because it played such a crucial role in the Athenians' construction of themselves, it remains one of the principal legacies of Greek civilization to western civilization and our own."[1]

Paying Tribute

One way that the people showed how important Athena was to them was by using the strongest and most expensive materials to build the monument. "The Parthenon was built completely of marble from the base of the temple to its roof tiles. It had two large-scale **pediments**, each filled with over twenty larger-than-life-sized marble figures in compositions that [praised] Athena and her power," states Hurwit.[2]

When most modern people think of the monuments built to honor Athena, they picture the Athena Parthenos, which was inside the Parthenon. But this wasn't the only—or even the most popular—statue of the goddess in ancient times. "Athena was known in many guises, and there were many Athenas worshipped on the **Acropolis**. The most sacred was not the Athena of the Parthenon," notes Hurwit. "It was, rather, an old olivewood statue of Athena called Athena Polias, referring to Athena as the guardian of the city. This little olivewood statue eventually inhabited the Erechtheum (ih-REK-thee-uhm), the classical temple of Athena Polias across from the Parthenon."[3]

But Hurwit concedes, "[T]he most glorious image of Athena, the one that expressed the power and wealth of Athens itself, was the Athena Parthenos, a colossal gold-and-ivory statue that Pheidias (FID-ee-uhs), supposedly the general overseer of the entire **Periclean** building program, created for the main room of the Parthenon. We call the Parthenon the Parthenon because of that statue, the Athena Parthenos . . . The statue seems to have been over twelve meters tall, nearly forty feet tall. The parts of her flesh that were visible were made of ivory, and her dress, her armor, and her jewelry were made of gold—some forty to forty-four talents of gold. A talent is approximately fifty-seven to fifty-eight pounds, and so the Athena wore on her body a tremendous sum and was the single greatest financial **asset** of the city."[4]

Erechtheum

Did That Really Happen?

Although it wasn't built to honor Athena, the work of art most often associated with her is the Trojan Horse. In the story about the Trojan War, Athena helped the Greeks win the war by assisting them in building a giant—and hollow—wooden horse. The Greeks left this horse outside the walls of Troy. It was a gift to the Trojans and a sign that the Greeks had given up and gone home. The Trojans accepted the gift and brought it inside the city, but the gift was not what it seemed. Hiding inside the horse were several Greek soldiers. At night, the soldiers crept out of the horse and unlocked the gates of Troy, allowing the rest of the Greek army to enter and destroy the city.

No one knows for certain whether this enormous structure truly ever existed or not. Some **archaeologists** devoted years to trying to prove that it did. They didn't find the Trojan horse, but they *did* find the ruins of the city of Troy. These ruins exist in multiple layers, indicating that the city was rebuilt many times. "Troy 6" and "Troy 7" are the layers that interest historians the most. While Troy 6 most closely matches Homer's description of Troy, this city was actually destroyed by an earthquake in 1250 BCE. A war in 1175 BCE was the downfall of the much smaller city of Troy 7. Some historians think that Homer may have used the Trojan horse as a symbol of Troy 6's earthquake. Archaeologist and historian Eric Cline offers another possibility. "Homer may have taken the description of Troy 6 and the destruction of Troy 7, and . . . blurred the two into one ten-year-long war," he says.[5]

Whether the Trojan War was real or imagined, Athena cared deeply about its outcome. She provided assistance when it was needed most to many of the Greek heroes

This replica of the Trojan Horse stands today at the site of Troy's ruins in Turkey.

in their fight. It is no secret, though, that her favorite was Odysseus.

And just like Athena, many fans of Greek mythology also have their favorites. For Rick Riordan, the goddess of wisdom makes his top two. He says it's no surprise that Athena and Poseidon are his favorite Greek goddess and god. "I've always been drawn to the power of the ocean, and Athena always [strikes] me as the most helpful goddess," he says.[6]

Although archaeology tells us that an earthquake destroyed the city of Troy, artists have embraced the idea that the city fell to flames during the Trojan War. The Burning of Troy by Johann Georg Trautmann is just one work of art depicting this event.

WINGED WISDOM

Athena hasn't just inspired great works of art in the city of Athens—or even only in the country of Greece. She is also depicted in many other places around the world. In Jacksonville, Florida, for example, visitors find one of her best-known symbols outside the city's library. Larry Kirkland is an artist from Washington, DC. He sculpted the twenty-five-foot owl that sits at the corner of the building. The bronze bird, which has been named Wisdom, weighs five tons, and is perched on a stack of books. A key adorned with the first and last letters of the Greek alphabet hangs above its head. It fits the lock on one of the books—a **figurative** key to knowledge.

"Kirkland got the idea to use the owl figure after extensive talks with people on the selection committee, who felt a classical female figure would be the right match for a traditional library," writes journalist Tanya Perez-Brennan. "After doing some research, he discovered that the Greek goddess Athena, protector of Athens, was often accompanied by an owl. According to Greek myth, she often transformed into one."[7]

"The whole idea of the owl goes back to Athena—he was her mascot," Kirkland said. "The owl symbolizes wisdom and intellectual **prowess**."[8]

Wisdom by Larry Kirkland at the Jacksonville, Florida, library

CHAPTER NOTES

Chapter 2: Stories Still Told

1. Frank Whelan, "Hollywood's Version of Homer's 'Iliad' Adds Some Mythology of its Own," *Morning Call*, May 23, 2004, http://articles.mcall.com/2004-05-23/entertainment/3538737_1_trojan-war-trojan-prince-paris-goddesses

2. Ibid.

3. Homer, *Iliad*, trans. Robert Fagles (New York: Viking Penguin, 1990), p. 243.

4. Ibid., p. 145.

5. Ibid., p. 146.

6. Ibid., p. 244.

7. Ibid., p. 243.

Chapter 3: A Long Journey Home

1. Homer, *Odyssey*, trans. Robert Fitzgerald (New York: Vintage Books, 1962), p. 3.

2. Ibid., p. 240.

3. Homer, *Odyssey*, trans. Allen Mandelbaum (New York: Bantam Classics, 1991), p. 491.

4. Ibid.

5. Ibid.

6. Kevin Canfield, "The Greek Myths Transcend the Ages," *Los Angeles Times*, March 30, 2001. http://articles.latimes.com/2001/mar/30/news/cl-44442

7. Ibid.

8. Ibid.

9. Ibid.

10. Paul Harris, "In Focus: Cinema: The Fempire Strikes Back," *The Observer*, January 29, 2012.

11. Ibid.

12. Ibid.

CHAPTER NOTES

Chapter 4: Passing Her Wisdom Down

1. Natalie Furman and Abby Semelsberger, "Chatting with the Stars of 'Percy Jackson,'" *Newsday*, August 6, 2013, http://long-island.newsday.com/kids/kidsday/chatting-with-the-stars-of-percy-jackson-1.5835527

2. Lauren R. Harrison, "Young Cast Takes on Classic Themes," *Chicago Tribune*, February 12, 2010.

3. Rick Riordan, *The Mark of Athena* (New York: Hyperion Books, 2012), p. 231.

4. Ibid., pp. 231–232.

5. Ibid., p. 405.

6. Ibid.

7. National Endowment for the Humanities, "It Came From Greek Mythology," September 30, 2010, http://edsitement.neh.gov/lesson-plan/it-came-greek-mythology

Chapter 5: Works of Art

1. Gary Glassman, interview with Jeffrey Hurwit, "The Glorious Parthenon," ed. Susan K. Lewis, PBS, NOVA, January 29, 2008, http://www.pbs.org/wgbh/nova/ancient/glorious-parthenon.html

2. Ibid.

3. Ibid.

4. Ibid.

5. Stefan Lovgren, "Is Troy True? The Evidence Behind Movie Myth," *National Geographic News*, May 14, 2004, http://news.nationalgeographic.com/news/2004/05/0514_040514_troy.html

6. Becky Scott, interview with Rick Riordan, *Bookette*, September 15, 2010, http://www.thebookette.co.uk/2010/09/author-interview-rick-riordan.html

7. Tanya Perez-Brennan, "5 Picked to Create Public Art," *Florida Times Union*, September 8, 2003.

8. Ibid.

WORKS CONSULTED

Bowman, Laurel, Anthony Bulloch, Andrew Campbell, Alys Caviness, Kathryn Chew, and Anna Claybourne. *Gods and Goddesses of Greece and Rome*. New York: Marshall Cavendish, 2011.

Buxton, Richard. *The Complete World of Greek Mythology*. London: Thames & Hudson, 2004.

Canfield, Kevin. "The Greek Myths Transcend the Ages." *Los Angeles Times*, March 30, 2001. http://articles.latimes.com/2001/ mar/30/news/cl-44442

Furman, Natalie, and Abby Semelsberger. "Chatting with the Stars of 'Percy Jackson.'" *Newsday*, August 6, 2013. http://long-island. newsday.com/kids/kidsday/chatting-with-the-stars-of-percy-jackson-1.5835527

Glassman, Gary. Interview with Jeffrey Hurwit. "The Glorious Parthenon." Edited by Susan K. Lewis. PBS, NOVA, January 29, 2008. http://www.pbs.org/wgbh/nova/ancient/glorious-parthenon.html

Hamilton, Edith. *Mythology: Timeless Tales of Gods and Heroes*. New York: Warner Books, 1999.

Harrison, Lauren R. "Young Cast Takes on Classic Themes." *Chicago Tribune*, February 12, 2010.

Harris, Paul. "In Focus: Cinema: The Fempire Strikes Back." *Observer*, January 29, 2012.

Homer. *Iliad*. Translated by Robert Fagles. New York: Viking Penguin, 1990.

Homer. *Odyssey*. Translated by Allen Mandelbaum. New York: Bantam Classics, 1991.

Homer. *Odyssey*. Translated by Robert Fitzgerald. New York: Vintage Books, 1962.

Louden, Bruce. *The Iliad: Structure, Myth, and Meaning*. Baltimore, MD: Johns Hopkins University Press, 2006.

Lovgren, Stefan. "Is Troy True? The Evidence Behind Movie Myth." *National Geographic News*, May 14, 2004. http://news. nationalgeographic.com/news/2004/05/0514_040514_troy.html

Mutén, Burleigh. *Goddesses: A World of Myth and Magic*. Cambridge, MA: Barefoot Books, 1997.

WORKS CONSULTED

Napoli, Donna Jo. *Treasury of Greek Mythology*. Washington, DC: National Geographic, 2011.

National Endowment for the Humanities. "It Came From Greek Mythology." September 30, 2010. http://edsitement.neh.gov/lesson-plan/it-came-greek-mythology

Perez-Brennan, Tanya. "5 Picked to Create Public Art." *Florida Times Union*, September 8, 2003.

Philip, Neil. *The Illustrated Book of Myths*. New York: DK Publishing, 1995.

Riordan, Rick. *The Mark of Athena*. New York: Hyperion Books, 2012.

Scott, Becky. Interview with Rick Riordan. *Bookette*, September 15, 2010. http://www.thebookette.co.uk/2010/09/author-interview-rick-riordan.html

Whelan, Frank. "Hollywood's Version of Homer's 'Iliad' Adds Some Mythology of its Own." *Morning Call*, May 23, 2004. http://articles.mcall.com/2004-05-23/entertainment/3538737_1_trojan-war-trojan-prince-paris-goddesses

FURTHER READING

Holub, Joan, and Suzanne Williams. *Athena the Brain*. New York: Aladdin, 2010.

Holub, Joan, and Suzanne Williams. *Athena the Wise*. New York: Aladdin, 2011.

O'Connor, George. *Athena: Grey-Eyed Goddess*. New York: First Second, 2010.

Riordan, Rick. *The Mark of Athena*. New York: Hyperion Books, 2012.

Sutcliff, Rosemary. *Black Ships Before Troy: The Story of the Iliad*. New York: Laurel-Leaf, 2005.

Glossary

Acropolis (uh-KROP-uh-lis)—the fortress of Athens which contains the Parthenon and other buildings

archaeologist (ahr-kee-OL-uh-jist)—a scientist who learns about prehistoric people by studying the things they left behind

asset (AS-et)—property that a person, business, or government has which has some value

bard (BAHRD)—a person in ancient societies who sang or recited poems about heroes

choreography (kawr-ee-OG-ruh-fee)—the art of arranging dances or other movements

contriver (kuhn-TRAHYV-er)—a person who plans in a skillful or clever way

counterpart (KOUN-ter-pahrt)—a person who performs a similar function or acts in a similar way as another person in another place

deception (dih-SEP-shuhn)—the act of misleading with intentional lies, trickery

demigod (DEM-ee-god)—one who is part god and part human

discord (DIS-kawrd)—lack of agreement or harmony; disagreement or conflict

embodiment (em-BOD-ee-muhnt)—the physical form of an idea or something else that is not normally physical

empower (em-POU-er)—to give power to

figurative (FIG-yer-uh-tiv)—representing an idea with a figure

Hydra (HAHY-druh)—a mythological serpent with nine heads

inadequate (in-AD-i-kwit)—not enough

irrational (ih-RASH-uh-nul)—not based on facts or reason

keen—eager

pediment (PED-uh-muhnt)—a triangular space forming the gable of a roof in classical architecture

Periclean (per-i-KLEE-uhn)—during the time of Athenian leader Pericles

phenomenon (fi-NOM-uh-non)—a remarkable or impressive fact or event

plethora (PLETH-er-uh)—overabundance, excess, or large number

plume (PLOOM)—a feather or tuft of feathers worn as decoration (as on a hat or helmet)

prowess (PROU-is)—exceptional skill or ability

rebellious (ri-BEL-yuhs)—resisting or going against authority

repository (ri-POZ-i-tawr-ee)—a storage place

resent (ri-ZENT)—to feel or show displeasure towards a person because of a past injury or insult

savage (SAV-ij)—fierce; uncivilized

trial (TRAHY-uhl)—a difficult test or challenge

trident (TRAHYD-nt)—a spear with three prongs

venomous (VEN-uh-muhs)—having or producing poison

INDEX

ABOUT THE
AUTHOR

Tammy Gagne is the author of numerous books for adults and children, including *Trends in Martial Arts* and *We Visit South Africa* for Mitchell Lane Publishers. She resides in northern New England with her husband and son. One of her favorite pastimes is visiting schools to speak to kids about the writing process.